WHY WAS THERE A CIVIL WAR?

US HISTORY 5TH GRADE CHILDREN'S AMERICAN HISTORY

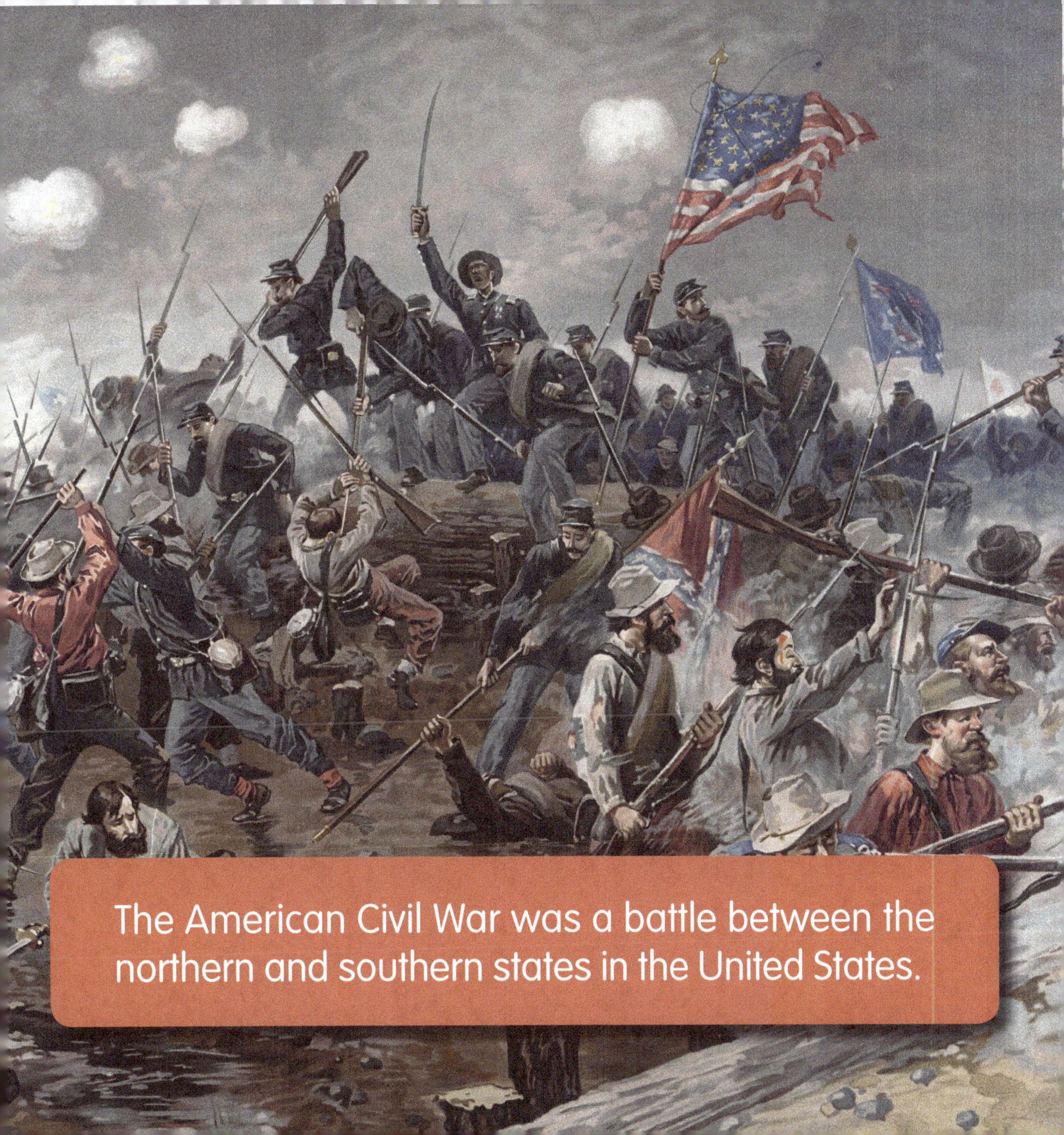

The American Civil War was a battle between the northern and southern states in the United States.

The southern states no longer wanted to be a part of the United States and wanted to create a country of their own. The northern states, however, wanted to remain as one country. Read further to learn about this war and the leaders.

BATTLE OF CHICKAMAUGA

BATTLE OF GETTYSBURG

THE SOUTH (CONFEDERACY)

Once the southern states made the decision to separate, or secede, they created the Confederate States of America, also known as the Confederacy. They had their own Constitution as well as president, Jefferson Davis. Tennessee, North Carolina, Arkansas, Virginia, Texas, Louisiana, Georgia, Alabama, Florida, Mississippi, and South Carolina were the 11 states that made up the Confederacy.

THE NORTH (UNION)

The 25 remaining states in the north made up the North, which was also known as the Union, symbolizing their desire to keep the Union States a single union and country. The North was had more industries and was larger than the South. They had a greater amount of wealth, resources, and people which gave them the advantage during this war.

CIVIL WAR CASUALTIES

WHY DID THE SOUTHERN STATES WANT TO LEAVE?

These states felt that while the United States continued to grow, they would lose power. They wanted to have separate laws and have greater power. The law they were mostly concerned about was regarding slavery. Slavery had already been outlawed in many of the northern states. The South worried that slavery would be outlawed throughout all states.

There are several reasons leading to the Civil War. Slavery may have been considered the main issue for this war, but there were other cultural and political differences that contributed as well. Read on to learn about these differences and the divide they creating eventually causing the war.

BATTE OF FRANKLIN
U.S.
U.S.

INDUSTRY VS. FARMING

Many of the northern states had moved from farming to industry during the mid-1800s. Many people living in the North worked in the larger cities, including Boston, Philadelphia, and New York. However, in the South, they remained as a larger farming economy, which utilized slave labor. The South continued to rely on slaves as a way of life, and the North no longer had a use for slaves.

STATES RIGHTS

The premise of the rights of states was not new. Arguments regarding power between the states and the power of the government had been ongoing since the Constitution was written. The South felt the government was taking their powers and rights.

CIVIL WAR ZOUAVE AMBULANCE

EXPANSION

While the United States continued its expansion west, with each additional state, the power was shifted between the North and South. The southern states feared that they would be losing too much power, including their rights. Any new state would soon be a battleground for power.

SLAVERY

Slavery was the heart of most of the South's issues. They relied on it as labor in the fields. Most of the North considered it evil and wrong. They were known as abolitionists. They wanted it to be illegal throughout the States.

ABOLITIONIST MEETING

Harriet Beecher Stowe, Harriet Tubman, Frederick Douglass, and John Brown were abolitionists that wanted to convince everyone of slavery's evils. The South feared this way of life would end.

BLEEDING KANSAS

The fight regarding slavery first occurred in Kansas. The government, in 1854, had passed the Kansas-Nebraska Act which allowed Kansas' residents the ability to vote on whether to be a free state or a slave state.

The region soon became flooded with people supporting both sides, and fought for years over this issue. Small skirmishes resulted in the deaths of many and the confrontation became known as Bleeding Kansas. In 1861, Kansas eventually joined the Union and became a free state.

ABRAHAM LINCOLN

The last straw in the South was when Abraham Lincoln was elected as President of the United States. He had been a member of the newly created anti-slavery Republican Party. He was able to be elected, even though he was not even on the ballot for ten of the southern states. They felt that since he was against slavery, he was against the South.

ABRAHAM LINCOLN

SECESSION

Once Lincoln became President, several southern states made the decision not to be associated with the United States any longer, and felt they had the right to leave.

Beginning with South Carolina, the eleven states eventually left the United States to form their own country known as the Confederate States of America. President Lincoln told them they could not leave and sent troops to prevent them from leaving. This was the beginning of the Civil War.

UNION GENERALS

ULYSSES S. GRANT

General Grant was the leader of the Army of Tennessee during the war's early stages. He claimed two early victories, Fort Henry and Fort Donelson, which earned him the nickname of "Unconditional Surrender." After major victories of Shiloh and Vicksburg, President Lincoln promoted him to lead the Union Army.

He then led the Army of the Potomac through several battles against the Confederate General Robert E. Lee, eventually accepting his surrender which occurred at Appomattox Court House.

ROBERT E. LEE

GEORGE MCCLELLAN

General McClellan was named as head over the Union Army of the Potomac following the First Battle of Bull Run. He was considered timid for a general. He thought he was outnumbered most of the time, when actually his army typically was larger than the Confederate army. He led their army during the Battle of Antietam, refusing to pursue the Confederates after this battle and was then relieved of his title.

General Sherman was the leader under Grant during the Siege of Vicksburg and the Battle of Shiloh. He then commanded his army and conquered Atlanta. He is most notorious for the "march to the sea" which proceeded from Atlanta to Savannah where he then destroyed anything that they could use against his army.

WILLIAM TECUMSEH SHERMAN

JOSEPH HOOKER

General Hooker led several major battles during the Civil War, which included the Battle of Fredericksburg and the Battle of Antietam. He was placed in command over the Army of the Potomac after Fredericksburg. However, he suffered a major defeat at the Battle of Chancellorsville and Abraham Lincoln relieved him of his command right before the Battle of Gettysburg.

General Hancock was known as one of the bravest and most talented commander of the Union Army. His command led over several battles, which included the Battle of Antietam, Battle of Gettysburg, and Battle of Spotsylvania Court House. He is most notorious for his leadership and bravery during the Battle of Gettysburg.

WINFIELD SCOTT HANCOCK

GEORGE THOMAS

General Thomas was considered to be one of the best Union generals. He won many important victories towards west. He is mostly known for his defense at the Battle of Chickamauga during which he was known as "the Rock of Chickamauga". In addition, he was able to lead the Union to victory during the Battle of Nashville.

CONFEDERATE GENERALS

General Lee was the leader of the Confederate Army of Virginia during the Civil War. He was an exceptional commander and won several battles even when outnumbered. The Second Battle of Bull Run, the Battle of Fredericksburg, and the Battle of Chancellorsville were some of his greater victories.

GENERAL LEE AT APPPOMATTOX COURT HOUSE

STONEWALL JACKSON

General Jackson became known as "Stonewall" during the First Battle of Bull Run, which occurred early during the war. As his soldiers held against a Union attack, it was told the he would stand like a "stone wall". He was also known for a fast paced "foot cavalry". He was victorious during many battles at the Shenandoah Valley during their Valley Campaign, but was killed accidentally during the Battle of Chancellorsville, sadly by his own men.

General Stuart (also referred to as "Jeb") was the Confederacy's lead cavalry commander. He fought during the First Battle of Bull Run, the Battle of Fredericksburg, and the Battle of Chancellorsville, and others. Even though he was considered a smart commander, he erred at the Battle of Gettysburg which may have resulted in the loss at this battle. He was killed during the Battle of Yellow Tavern.

J.E.B. STUART

P.G.T. BEAUREGARD

General Beauregard was able to lead the South during the capture of Fort Sumter. He then fought the battles of Shiloh and Bull Run. His renowned ability to hold off the Union forces at St. Petersburg while waiting for cavalries from Robert E. Lee is probably his greatest accomplishment.

It was General Johnston that lead the Confederates to their first big win at the First Battle of Bull Run. Unfortunately, he and President Jefferson David could not agree, and he then suffered some losses while commanding towards the west, which included the battles at Chickamauga and Vicksburg. He and his army then surrendered to General Sherman which ended the Civil War.

JOSEPH JOHNSTON

BATTLE OF WILSON'S CREEK

THE FIGHTING

The Civil War would end up to be the most deadly war in American history. More than 600,000 soldiers lost their lives during this war. It began on April 12, 1861, at Fort Sumter in South Carolina and ended as General Lee surrendered to Grant on April 9, 1865 in Virginia, at the Appomattox Court House.

For additional information on the Civil War research the internet, go to your local library, and ask questions of your teacher, family, and friends.

BATTLE OF FORT DONELSON

Visit
BABY PROFESSOR
EDUCATION KIDS
www.BabyProfessorBooks.com
to download Free Baby Professor eBooks
and view our catalog of new and exciting
Children's Books

9 798869 432957